God's *Judgment* on the Nations

Compiled By Rev. Kaatee Bailey

God's *Judgment* on the Nations

Other Books by Rev. Kaatee Bailey
Israel's Biblical Right to the Land

Other Books Soon Available:
Israel's Historical Rights to the Land
Israel's Legal Rights to the Land
Israel's Archaeological Rights to the Land

This book of accumulated Scriptures, compiled by Rev. Kaatee Bailey, is a reference guide regarding the 'Judgment of God' on the nations who mistreat Israel and the Jewish People. The Scriptures affirm that God in His justice will bring vengeance on Israel's enemies. The Scripture quotations used are from various easy to read translations of the Holy Bible. The books of the Bible used are written in English and Hebrew.

Copyright 2013 First Printing
Published by The Hawaii-Israel Alignment
ISBN 0615915167

God's *Judgment* on the Nations

As you have done to Israel,

so it will be done to you.

All your evil deeds

will fall back on your own heads.

Obadiah 1:15

Forward

This book clearly depicts the coming judgment to all nations that have despised the Nation of Israel, the apple of God's eye. My prayer is that you will take this to heart. The decision is in your hands. How will you treat the Nation of Israel and the Jewish People? "I will bless those that bless you and curse those who curse you and all the families of the earth will be blessed because of you. (Genesis 12:3)

Thank you Kaatee for your insight concerning Israel and the judgment on the nations. I am grateful for your unwavering commitment and your zealous love for Israel. May Yeshua richly bless and protect you all your days.

Nowlin Correa
Founder of Khiilat HaMishkan Ministries
Co-coordinator of 'The Hawaii-Israel Alignment'

Introduction

Joel 3:1-2 "For behold, in those days and at that time when I shall reverse the captivity and restore the fortunes of Judah and Jerusalem, I will gather all nations and will bring them down into the Valley of Jehoshaphat, and there will I deal with and execute judgment upon them for their treatment of My people and of My heritage Israel, whom they have scattered among the nations and because they have divided My land."

The word 'nations' translated into Hebrew is 'Goyim', a term that signifies a non-Hebrew people or the Gentile Nations. Distinctly, the Prophet Joel is describing how God will gather the non-Hebrew People of all nations in the Valley of Jehoshaphat to be judged. This assembly of people will include all nations on the globe including America. No Gentile people-group will be excluded from this day marked on God's calendar. There in the Valley of Jehoshaphat they will all be judged. The name 'Jehoshaphat' has a prophetic message in context with these verses. It means 'Yahweh judges.' Yahweh will judge the Gentile nations and execute His judgment. What will determine God's judgment on these nations? *"There I will execute judgment upon them for the treatment of my people... and because they have divided my land" (Joel 1:2).* The Prophet Joel leaves no room for doubt concerning this judgment day. This decree is clearly based on the treatment of God's Chosen People and their land.

Jesus expounds in further detail about the 'Judgment on the

Nations' in Matthew 25:31-46. When Jesus returns in all his glory, the nations will be gathered before Him. He will separate the sheep nations on the right and the goat nations on His left. Their judgment will be determined by the way they treated the Jewish People. Jesus said, *"Inasmuch as ye have done it unto one of the least of these my brethren, ye have done it unto me."* (Verse 40) The expression, *"least of these my brethren"* from the Greek translation is a term that refers to 'relatives according to the flesh.' Jesus's ethnic background is Jewish and His relatives according to the flesh are the Jewish People.

Jesus told his disciples, "I was hungry and you didn't feed me. I was thirsty and you didn't give me water. I was naked and you didn't clothe me." They replied, "When did we see you in that condition?" Jesus responded that it was whenever they saw one of his 'relatives' in these conditions.

During the Holocaust, many people and nations turned their backs to the relatives of Jesus. They remained silent and did not speak out on their behalf. They did nothing to help them. There was no support, no comfort nor any kind of assistance made for them. The world watched six million Jews plus children die under tormenting circumstances. They closed their eyes to their pain and their ears to their cries. Being a by stander is as serious as one committing a crime. Jesus concludes His words in **Mathew 25:45** by saying, *"The truth is, anything you refuse to do for any of my people here, you refuse to do for me."*

God cares deeply for His relatives and He takes it very personally how one treats His family members. While He certainly loves all

Inhabitants of the earth, God chose the Jewish People to be His treasured possession. They are very dear and tender to His heart. We cannot love the God of Israel and not love His chosen people. The Prophet Zechariah tells us, *"For he who touches you, touches the apple of His eye" (Zechariah 2:8).* In Hebrew, the phrase *"apple of His eye"* refers to the pupil of God's eye. When someone touches a Jew, they are touching God's pupil. The pupil is one of the most sensitive parts of the human anatomy. When you touch a Jew, you are touching something very sensitive to God's heart.

Mistreating the relatives of Jesus is a grave matter to God. Let there be no doubt, He will judge those who harm His family members. The nations will be judged based on their treatment of the Jewish People.

The nation of Egypt was judged for enslaving the Israelites, killing Jewish baby boys, and for their cruelty to the people of Israel. God brought the ten plagues against ancient Egypt which resulted in unprecedented destruction to the country. God sent judgments upon Egypt far beyond any expectation.

The Assyrian Empire came face to face with God's judgment for their cruelty to the Jewish people and the destruction of their land. They were the crudest nation of antiquity and devastated the land of Israel, first by taking the northern section into captivity and eventually, the southern segment. The Assyrians captured all of the 46 fortified cities of Israel except a small fracture of Jerusalem. Everything else was devastated. Their massive cruelty upon God's People and their land incurred God's judgment on their own land.

The prophet Zephaniah spoke of those days: ***"And He will stretch out His hand against the north, destroy Assyria, and make Nineveh desolate, as dry as the wilderness" (Zeph. 2:13).*** In 612 BC, Nineveh, the capital city of Assyria, was completely destroyed and leveled to the ground. All that remains of that once great city are a few mounds of dirt in what is now Iraq. Assyria vanished from the face of the globe.

What happened to Haman, the conspirator of an evil plan to exterminate Mordecai and all the Jews in ancient Persia? His plot backfired, and the sentence he planned for them fell on him and his sons. ***What he intended to do to them was done to him. Haman and his sons were hung on the very gallows he had prepared for Mordecai (Esther7:10   Esther 9:24-25).***

God, the One who does what He says He will, in His justice judged these and other nations and cities throughout the Bible. They were judged for how they treated Israel and the Jewish people.

The words of the Prophet Obadiah re-affirm God's vengeance on those who oppress his people. He is speaking to Edom. ***"You will be covered with shame because you were very cruel to your brother Jacob. So you will be destroyed completely. You joined the enemies of Israel. Strangers carried Israel's treasures away. Foreigners entered Israel's city gate. They threw lots to decide what part of Jerusalem they would get. And you were right there with them, waiting to get your share. You should not have laughed at your brother's trouble. You should not have been*** *happy when they destroyed Judah. You should not have bragged at the time of their trouble. You should not have entered the city gate of my people and laughed at their problems. You should not have taken their treasures in the time of their trouble. You should not have stood where the roads cross and destroyed those who were trying to escape. You should not have captured those who escaped alive. The Day of the Lord is coming soon to all the nations. As you have done to Israel, so shall it be done onto you. Your acts will return upon your own head. (Obadiah 1:10-15)*

We should not take God's words carelessly when it comes to the treatment of His family members. He means what He says. We are nearing the time when God will avenge these nations for mistreating His people, for scattering them and for dividing His land.

The Prophet Joel tells us, **"there are *"multitudes, multitudes in the Valley of Decision" (Joel 3:14).*** We are living in the time period when the non- Hebrew People Nations are making a decision. They are determining their fate. Some will be sheep nations destined for blessing and some will be goat nations destined for judgment. Our lands need to choose God's plan for blessing, and turn away from the path that leads to judgment and possible destruction.

From the Biblical declarations of God's love and care for His chosen people, and from the history of the nation's being destroyed because of their evil dealings with Israel, Christians must wake up to this urgent hour of decision. It is not time to remain silent or inactive concerning Israel. Silence allows unrighteousness and evil to reign. Albert Einstein once said, "The world is a dangerous place not because of those who do evil, but because of those who look on and do nothing. If you don't speak, you're making a statement. If you don't stand up, you're taking a position." We must be active about issues that are important to God.

God's character is one of mercy, justice and longsuffering. He is allowing us a fresh opportunity to join His efforts for His eternal plan and purpose for Israel. By blessing Abraham's seed, we are closing the door that leads to judgment and destruction and opening the door to the path destined for blessing. *In Abraham's seed all the nations will be blessed (Genesis 22:18).*

It is my duty and call to America and the Nations across the globe to STAND UP FOR ISRAEL. Let us all cooperate and combine our forces to be an active partner with God in His great plan and purpose for Israel and the Jewish People!

.

Genesis – B'resheet

Genesis12:2-3 (King James Bible)

"I will make you a great nation; I will bless you and make your name great; and you shall be a blessing. **I will bless those who bless you, and I will curse him who curses you;** and in you all the families of the earth shall be blessed."

Deuteronomy – D'varim

Deuteronomy 30:7-9   (Living Bible)

"If you return to the Lord and obey all the commandments that I command you today, **the Lord your God will take his curses and turn them against your enemies, against those who hate you and persecute you.** The Lord your God will prosper everything you do and give you many children and much cattle and wonderful crops; for the Lord will again rejoice over you as he did over your fathers.

Deuteronomy 32:43   (Good News Translation)

"Nations, you must praise the Lord's people—**he punishes all who kill them. He takes revenge on his enemies** and forgives the sins of his people."

Psalms – Tehillim

Psalms 83:1-13 (Easy to Read Version)

God, don't keep quiet! Don't close your ears! Please say something, God. **Your enemies** are getting ready to do something. Those who hate you will soon attack. They **are making secret plans against your people. Your enemies are discussing plans against the people you love**. They say, "Come, let us destroy them completely. Then no one will ever again remember the name Israel." God, they have all joined together. They have united against you. Their army includes the Edomites, Ishmaelites, Moabites, and Hagar's descendants, the people of Byblos, Ammon, and Amalek, the Philistines, and the people of Tyre. Even the Assyrians have joined them. They have made Lot's descendants very powerful. Selah. **God, defeat them just as you defeated Midian. Do what you did to Sisera and Jabin at the Kishon River. You destroyed the enemy at Endor, and their bodies rotted on the ground. Punish their leaders as you did Oreb and Zeeb. Do what you did to Zebah and Zalmunna. May those who hate Zion be put to shame. May they be stopped and chased away. They will be like grass on a flat roof that dies before It has time to grow.**

Psalms 129:5-7 (New International Version)

<u>May all who hate Zion be turned back in shame.</u> May they be like grass on the roof, which withers before it can grow; a reaper cannot fill his hands with it, nor one who gathers fill his arms.

Psalms 136:11- (Easy to Read Version)

<u>He took Israel out of Egypt</u>. His faithful love will last forever. He used his powerful arms and strong hands. His faithful love will last forever. <u>He split the Red Sea into two parts</u>. His faithful love will last forever. He led Israel through the sea. His faithful love will last forever. <u>He drowned Pharaoh and his army in the Red Sea.</u> His faithful love will last forever. He led his people through the desert. His faithful love will last forever. <u>He defeated powerful kings.</u> His faithful love will last forever.

Isaiah – Yesha'yahu

Isaiah 41:8-12   (New American Standard)

"But you, Israel, My servant, Jacob whom I have chosen, Descendant of Abraham My friend, You whom I have taken from the ends of the earth, And called from its remotest parts And said to you, 'You are My servant, I have chosen you and not rejected you. 'Do not fear, for I am with you; do not anxiously look about you, for I am your God. I will strengthen you, surely I will help you. Surely I will uphold you with My righteous right hand.' **"Behold, all those who are angered at you will be shamed and dishonored; those who contend with you will be as nothing and will perish. "You will seek those who quarrel with you, but will not find them, those who war with you will be as nothing and non-existent."**

Isaiah 43:14-15   (New American Standard)

Thus says the Lord your Redeemer, the Holy One of Israel, **"For your sake I have sent to Babylon, and will bring them all down as fugitives, Even the Chaldeans, into the ships in which they rejoice.** "I am the Lord, your Holy One, The Creator of Israel, your King."

Isaiah 49:3, 25-26 (New International Version)

He said to me, "You are my servant, Israel, in whom I will display my splendor." **I will contend with those who contend with you,** and your children I will save. **I will make your oppressors eat their own flesh; they will be drunk on their own blood, as with wine.** Then all mankind will know that I, the Lord, am your Savior, your Redeemer, the Mighty One of Jacob."

Isaiah 51: 7-8 (New King James Version)

"Listen to Me, you who know righteousness, You people in whose heart is My law: **Do not fear the reproach of men, nor be afraid of their insults. For the moth will eat them up like a garment, and the worm will eat them like wool**; But My righteousness will be forever, and My salvation from generation to generation."

Isaiah 51:22- 23   (Easy to Read Version)

Your God is the one who fights for his people. He is your Lord God, and he says to you, "Look, **I am taking this 'cup of poison' away from you.** It is full of my anger, and I am taking it out of your hand. You will not be punished by my anger again. **I will now use my anger to punish the people who hurt you.** They tried to kill you." They told you, "Bow down before us, and we will walk on you." They forced you to bow down before them, and then they walked on your back like dirt. You were like a road for them to walk on.

Isaiah 54:14-17 (New American Standard)

In righteousness you will be established; you will be far from oppression, for you will not fear; and from terror, for it will not come near you. "If anyone fiercely assails you it will not be from Me. **Whoever assails you will fall because of you.** "Behold, I Myself have created the smith who blows the fire of coals and brings out a weapon for its work; and I have created the destroyer to ruin. "**No weapon that is formed against you will prosper; and every tongue that accuses you in judgment you will condemn.** This is the heritage of the servants of the Lord, and their vindication is from Me," declares the Lord.

Isaiah 60:12 (Living Bible)

For the nations refusing to be your allies will perish; they shall be destroyed.

Isaiah 60:14 (English Standard Version)

The sons of those who afflicted you shall come bending low to you, and all who despised you shall bow down at your feet; they shall call you the City of the Lord, the Zion of the Holy One of Israel.

Jeremiah - Yirmehyahu

Jeremiah 2:3 (Living Bible)

In those days Israel was a holy people, the first of my children. <u>All who harmed them were counted deeply guilty, and great evil fell on anyone who touched them.</u>

Jeremiah 10:25 (New International Version)

<u>Pour out your wrath on the nations</u> that do not acknowledge you, on the peoples who do not call on your name. <u>For they have devoured Jacob; they have devoured him completely and destroyed his homeland.</u>

Jeremiah 12:14 (New International Version)

This is what the LORD says: **"<u>As for all my wicked neighbors who seize the inheritance I gave my people Israel, I will uproot them from their lands</u>** and I will uproot the people of Judah from among them."

Jeremiah 24:8-10 (Easy to Read Version)

The Lord says, "I will treat King Zedekiah of Judah like those figs that are too rotten to eat. Zedekiah, his high officials, all those who are left in Jerusalem, and those people of Judah who are living in Egypt will be like those rotten figs. I will punish them. Their punishment will shock all the people on earth. **People will make fun of those people from Judah. People will tell jokes about them and curse them in all the places where I scatter them. I will bring war, famine, and disease against them. I will attack them until they have all been killed. Then they will no longer be on the land that I gave to them and to their ancestors."**

Jeremiah 25:12-14 (Easy to Read Version)

"But when the 70 years have passed, I will punish the king of Babylon. "I will punish the nation of Babylon." This message is from the Lord. "I will punish the land of the Babylonians for their sins. I will make that land a desert forever. **I said many bad things will happen to Babylon, and all of them will happen.** Jeremiah spoke about those foreign nations. And all the warnings are written in this book. Yes, the people of Babylon will have to serve many nations and many great kings. **I will give them the punishment they deserve for all the things they have done.**

Jeremiah 29:29-32 (English Standard Version)

Zephaniah the priest read this letter in the hearing of Jeremiah the prophet. Then the word of the Lord came to Jeremiah: "Send to all the exiles, saying, Thus says the Lord **concerning Shemaiah of Nehelam: Because Shemaiah had prophesied to you (Israel) when I did not send him, and has made you trust in a lie, therefore thus says the Lord: Behold, I will punish Shemaiah of Nehelam and his descendants.** He shall not have anyone living among this people, and he shall not see the good that I will do to my people, declares the Lord, for he has spoken rebellion against the Lord."

Jeremiah 30:11 (Easy to Read Version)

"**People of Israel and Judah**, I am with you." This message is from the Lord. "I will save you. I sent you to those nations, but **I will completely destroy all of them**. It is true; **I will destroy those nations, but I will not destroy you.**"

Jeremiah 30:16-17 (Good News Translation)

But now, all who devour you will be devoured, and all your enemies will be taken away as prisoners. All who oppress you will be oppressed, and all who plunder you will be plundered. I will make you well again; I will heal your wounds though your enemies say, 'Zion is an outcast; no one cares about her.' I, the Lord, have spoken.

Jeremiah 30:20 (Easy to Read Version)

Jacob's family will be like the family of Israel long ago. "**I will make Israel and Judah strong and I will punish those who hurt them.**"

Jeremiah 50:1-3, 9-13 (Easy to Read Version)

This is the message the Lord spoke through the prophet Jeremiah about Babylon and its people. Announce this to all nations. Lift up a flag and announce the message! Speak the whole message and say, "The nation of Babylon will be captured. The god Baal will be put to shame. The god Marduk will be very afraid. Babylon's idols will be put to shame. Her gods will be filled with terror. A nation from the north will attack Babylon. That nation will make Babylon like an empty desert. No one will live there. I will bring many nations together from the north. This group of nations will get ready for war against Babylon. Babylon will be captured by people from the north. Those nations will shoot many arrows at Babylon. Their arrows will be like soldiers who don't come back from war with their hands empty. The enemy will take all the wealth from the Chaldeans. The soldiers will take all they want." **This is what the Lord said. "Babylon, you are excited and happy. You took my land. You dance around like a young cow that got into the grain. Your laughter is like the happy sounds that horses make. Now your mother will be very ashamed. The woman who gave you birth will be embarrassed. Babylon will be the least important of all the nations. She will be an empty, dry desert. The Lord will show his anger, so no one**

will live there. **Babylon will be completely empty**. Everyone who passes by Babylon will be afraid. **They will shake their heads when they see how badly it has been destroyed.**

Jeremiah 50:17-18 (Easy to Read Version)

"Israel is like a flock of sheep that was scattered all over the country. Israel is like sheep that were chased away by lions. The first lion to attack was the king of Assyria. The last lion to crush Israel's bones was King Nebuchadnezzar of Babylon. **So this is what the Lord All-Powerful, the God of Israel, says: "I will soon punish the king of Babylon and his country as I punished the king of Assyria."**

Ezekiel – Yechezkel

Ezekiel 25:1-7   (Good News Translation)
(Prophecy against Ammon)

The Lord spoke to me. " Mortal man," he said, "**denounce the country of Ammon.**" Tell them to listen to what I, the Sovereign Lord, am saying: "**You were delighted to see my Temple profaned, to see the land of Israel devastated, and to see the people of Judah go into exile. Because you were glad, I will let the tribes from the eastern desert conquer you.** They will set up their camps in your country and settle there. They will eat the fruit and drink the milk that should have been yours. I will turn the city of Rabbah into a place to keep camels, and the whole country of Ammon will become a place to keep sheep, so that you will know I am the Lord." This is what the Sovereign Lord is saying: "**You clapped your hands and jumped for joy. You despised the land of Israel. Because you did, I will hand you over to other nations who will rob you and plunder you. I will destroy you so completely that you will not be a nation any more or have a country of your own.** Then you will know that I am the Lord."

Ezekiel 25: 8-11   (Good News Translation)
(Prophecy against Moab)
The Sovereign Lord said, "Because Moab has said that Judah is

like all the other (heathen) nations, I will let the cities that defend the border of Moab be attacked, including even the finest cities—Beth Jeshimoth, Baal Meon, and Kiriathaim. I will let the tribes of the eastern desert conquer Moab, together with Ammon, so that Moab will no longer be a nation. I will punish Moab, and they will know that I am the Lord."

Ezekiel 25:12-14 (Good News Translation)
(Prophecy against Edom)

The Sovereign Lord said, "The people of Edom took cruel revenge on Judah, and that revenge has brought lasting guilt on Edom. Now I announce that I will punish Edom and kill every person and animal there. I will make it a wasteland, from the city of Teman to the city of Dedan, and the people will be killed in battle. My people Israel will take revenge on Edom for me, and they will make Edom feel my furious anger. Edom will know what it means to be the object of my revenge." The Sovereign Lord has spoken.

Ezekiel 25: 15-17 (Message Bible)
(Prophecy against Philistia)

"God, the Master, says: Because the Philistines were so spitefully vengeful—all those centuries of stored-up malice!— and did their best to destroy Judah, therefore I, God, the Master, will oppose the Philistines and cut down the Cretans and anybody else left along the seacoast. Huge acts of vengeance, massive punishments! When I bring vengeance, they'll realize that I am God."

Ezekiel 35:1-9   (Good News Translation)

(Prophecy against Edom)

The Lord spoke to me. "Mortal man," he said, "denounce the country of Edom". Tell the people what I, the Sovereign Lord, am saying: **"I am your enemy, mountains of Edom! I will make you a desolate wasteland. I will leave your cities in ruins and your land desolate;** then you will know that I am the Lord." **"You were Israel's constant enemy and let her people be slaughtered in the time of her disaster, the time of final punishment for her sins. So then—as surely as I, the Sovereign Lord, am the living God— death is your fate, and you cannot escape it. You are guilty of murder, and murder will follow you. I will make the hill country of Edom a wasteland and kill everyone who travels through it. I will cover the mountains with corpses, and the bodies of those who are killed in battle will cover the hills and valleys. I will make you desolate forever, and no one will live in your cities again. Then you will know that I am the Lord."**

Ezekiel 35:10-11   (Good News Translation)

"You said that the two nations, Judah and Israel, together with their lands, belonged to you and that you would possess them,

even though I, the Lord, was their God. So then, as surely as I, the Sovereign Lord, I the living God, **I will pay you back for your anger, your jealousy, and your hate toward my people.** They will know that **I am punishing you for what you did to them.**"

Ezekiel 35:12-15 (Good News Translation)

I, the Lord, heard you say with contempt that the mountains of Israel were desolate and that they were yours to devour. I have heard the wild, boastful way you have talked against me. **The Sovereign Lord says, "I will make you so desolate that the whole world will rejoice at your downfall, just as you rejoiced at the devastation of Israel, my own possession.** The mountains of Seir, yes, **all the land of Edom, will be desolate.** Then everyone will know that I am the Lord."

Ezekiel 36:1-7 (Living Bible)

"Son of dust," prophesy to Israel's mountains. Tell them: "Listen to this message from the Lord. Your enemies have sneered at you and claimed your ancient heights as theirs; they have destroyed you on every side and sent you away as slaves to many lands. You are mocked and slandered. Therefore, **O mountains of Israel,** hear the word of the Lord God. He says to the hills and mountains, dales and valleys, and to the ruined farms and the long-deserted cities, **destroyed and mocked by heathen nations all around: My anger is afire against these nations, especially Edom, for grabbing my land with relish, in utter contempt for me, to take it**

for themselves. "Therefore prophesy and say to the hills and mountains, dales and valleys of Israel:" 'This is what the Lord God says! **"I am full of fury because you suffered shame before the surrounding nations. Therefore, I have sworn with hand held high that those nations are going to have their turn of being covered with shame."**

Ezekiel 38:17-23 (Living Bible)

The Lord God says: "You are the one I spoke of long ago through the prophets of Israel, saying that after many years had passed, I would bring you against my people. **But when you come to destroy the land of Israel, my fury will rise!** For in my jealousy and blazing wrath, I promise a mighty shaking in the land of Israel on that day. All living things shall quake in terror at my presence; mountains shall be thrown down; cliffs shall tumble; walls shall crumble to the earth. **I will summon every kind of terror against you," says the Lord God, "and you will fight against yourselves in mortal combat! I will fight you with sword, disease, torrential floods, great hailstones, fire, and brimstone! Thus will I show my greatness and bring honor upon my name, and all the Nations of the world will hear what I have done and know that I am God!"**

Ezekiel 39:1-8 (Living Bible)

"Son of dust, prophesy this also against Gog. Tell him: "I stand against you, Gog, leader of Meshech and Tubal. I will turn you and drive you toward the mountains of Israel, bringing you from the distant north. And I will destroy 85 percent of your army in the mountains. I will knock your weapons from your hands and leave you helpless. You and all your vast armies will die upon the mountains. I will give you to the vultures and wild animals to devour you. You will never reach the cities—you will fall upon the open fields; for I have spoken, the Lord God says. And I will rain down fire on Magog and on all your allies who live safely on the coasts, and they shall know I am the Lord. "**Thus I will make known my holy name among my people Israel; I will not let it be mocked at anymore.** And the nations, too, shall know I am the Lord, the Holy One of Israel. **That day of judgment will come; everything will happen just as I have declared it.**

Joel – Yo'el

Joel 3:1-3 (Easy to Read Version)

"Yes, at that time I will bring back the people of Judah and Jerusalem from captivity. I will also gather all the nations together. **I will bring all these nations down into Jehoshaphat Valley. There I will judge them. Those nations scattered my people, Israel. They forced them to live in other nations, so I will punish those nations. They divided up my land. They threw lots for my people. They sold boys to buy a prostitute, and they sold girls to buy wine to drink.**

Joel 3:4-8 (Easy to Read Version)

"Tyre! Sidon! All of you areas of Philistia! You are not important to me! Are you punishing me for something I did? You might think that you are punishing me, but **I will soon punish you. You took my silver and gold. You took my precious treasures and put them in your temples. "You sold the people of Judah and Jerusalem to the Greeks.** That way you could take them far from their land. **You sent my people to that faraway place**, but I will bring them back. **And I will punish you for what you did. I will sell your sons and daughters to the people of Judah.** Then they will sell them to the faraway Sabeans." This is what the Lord said.

Joel 3:19-21 (Easy to Read Version)

Egypt will be empty. Edom will be an empty wilderness, because they were cruel to the people of Judah. They killed innocent people in their country. But there will always be people living in Judah. People will live in Jerusalem through many generations. **Those people killed my people, so I really will punish them.** The Lord God will live in Zion!

Obadiah – Ovadyah

Obadiah 1:8- 10   (Easy to Read Version)

The Lord says, "On that day I will destroy the wise people from Edom. I will destroy the intelligent people from the mountain of Esau. Teman, your brave soldiers will be afraid. Everyone will be destroyed from the mountain of Esau. Many people will be killed. **You will be covered with shame because you were very cruel to your brother Jacob. So you will be destroyed completely.**

Obadiah 1:11 -15 (Easy to Read Version)

You joined the enemies of Israel. Strangers carried Israel's treasures away. Foreigners entered Israel's city gate. They threw lots to decide what part of Jerusalem they would get. And you were right there with them, waiting to get your share. **You should not have laughed at your brother's trouble. You should not have been happy when they destroyed Judah. You should not have bragged at the time of their trouble. You should not have entered the city gate of my people and laughed at their problems. You should not have taken their treasures in the time of their trouble. You should not have stood where the roads cross and destroyed those who were trying to escape. You should not have captured those who escaped alive.** The Lord's vengeance will soon fall on the Gentile nations; As **you have done to Israel, so shall it be done onto you. The same bad things will fall down on your own head.**

Zephaniah – Tz'fanyah

Zephaniah 2:8-10 (Easy to Read Version)

"**I have heard the insults of Moab and the taunts of the Ammonites, who insulted my people and made threats against their land.** Therefore, as surely as I live," declares the Lord Almighty the God of Israel, "surely Moab will become like Sodom, the Ammonites like Gomorrah—a place of weeds and salt pits, a wasteland forever. **The remnant of my people will plunder them; the survivors of my nation will inherit their land.**" **This is what they will get in return for their pride, for insulting and mocking the people of the Lord Almighty.**

Zephaniah 3:18-19 (New International Version)

"I will remove from you all who mourn over the loss of your appointed festivals, which is a burden and reproach for you. **At that time I will deal with all who oppressed you.**

Zechariah – Z'kharyah

Zechariah 2:7-9   (Easy to Read Version)

<u>You people from Zion now live in Babylon. **Escape! Run away from that city!**</u> **The Lord sent me to the nations that took away your wealth.** He sent me to bring you honor. And this is what the Lord All-Powerful said: **"If anyone even touches you, it is as if they did it to the pupil of my eye."** <u>Watch and see how I will punish them: Their own slaves will become their masters and take all their wealth.</u>" Then you will know it was the Lord All-Powerful who sent me to tell you these things.

Zechariah 9:1-8   (Easy to Read Version)

<u>This is the Lord's message against the land of Hadrach and against the city of Damascus.</u> The tribes of Israel are not the only people who know about the Lord. Everyone looks to him for help. This message is also **against the city of Hamath near Damascus.** And this message is **against Tyre and Sidon**, even though those people have been so wise and skillful. Tyre is built like a fort. The people there have collected so much silver that it is like dust, and gold is as common as clay. But the Lord will take it all. <u>He will destroy her powerful navy and that city will be destroyed by fire! The people in Ashkelon will see this and they will be afraid.</u>

The **people of Gaza will shake with fear, and the people of Ekron will lose all hope** when they see this happen. **There will be no king left in Gaza. No one will live in Ashkelon anymore.** The people in Ashdod will not even know who their real fathers are. The Lord says, "**I will completely destroy the proud Philistines.** They will no longer eat meat with the blood still in it or any other forbidden food. Any Philistine left alive will become a part of my people; they will be just one more tribe in Judah. The people of Ekron will become a part of my people, as the Jebusites did. **I will protect my country. I will not let enemy armies pass through it. I will not let them hurt my people anymore. With my own eyes I have seen how much my people have suffered.**"

Zechariah 12:1-5 (Easy to Read Version)

This is a message from the Lord about Israel. The Lord is the one who made the earth and the sky, and he put the human spirit in people. And this is what the Lord said: "Look, **I will make Jerusalem like a cup of poison to the nations around her. The nations will come and attack that city, and all of Judah will be caught in the trap. But I will make Jerusalem like a heavy rock—those who try to take it will hurt themselves. They will be cut and scratched. All the nations on earth will come together to fight against Jerusalem. But at that time I will scare the horse, and the soldier riding it will panic. I will make all the enemy horses blind, but my eyes will be open—and I will be watching over Judah's family**. The leaders of Judah will encourage the people and say, 'The Lord All-Powerful is your God. He makes us strong."

Zechariah 12:9 (American Standard Version)

And it shall come to pass in that day, that I will seek to destroy all the nations that come against Jerusalem.

Zechariah 14:2-3 (Living Bible)

Watch, for the day of the Lord is coming soon! On that day the Lord will gather together the nations to fight Jerusalem; the city will be taken, the houses rifled, the loot divided, the women raped; half the population will be taken away as slaves, and half will be left in what remains of the city. Then the Lord will go out fully armed for war, to fight against those nations.

Zechariah 14:12 (Living Bible)

And the Lord will send a plague on all the people who fought Jerusalem. They will become like walking corpses, their flesh rotting away; their eyes will shrivel in their sockets, and their tongues will decay in their mouths.

Contact us if you are Interested in:

- Participating in Kehilat HaMishkan Ministry in Hawaii

- Participating in the 'Hawaii-Israel Alignment'

- Participating in the 'America-Israel Alignment' (Align your State with Israel)

- Participating in a Gideon's Army of 300 Shofar Blowers to Jerusalem

- Planting an Olive Tree in Israel from your Hawaii District

- Financially Supporting the Hawaii-Israel Alignment (HIA)

- The Hawaii House Embassy in Jerusalem

- The Israeli House Embassy in Hawaii

The Hawaii - Israel Alignment
www. khmhawaii.com
41-050 Kalanianaole Hwy. Waimanalo, HI 96795

nowlincorrea@yahoo.com   shalommaui@aol.com
Oahu   808-330-8893   Maui 808-357-3303

www.ingramcontent.com/pod-product-compliance
Lightning Source LLC
Chambersburg PA
CBHW071759020426
42331CB00008B/2324